THE TOWER

Stephen Brooke

Arachis Press 2015

For I dream, and dream again.

The Tower
©2015 Stephen Brooke

All rights reserved. The text, art and design of this publication are the copyrighted work of Stephen Brooke and may not be reproduced nor transmitted in any form without the express written permission of the author or publisher, other than short quotes for review purposes.

ISBN 978-1-937745-27-1

Arachis Press
4803 Peanut Road
Graceville, FL 32440
http://arachispress.com

The Tower

I. The Keep

I dream and dream again the keep,
on my horizon ever brooding:
Polyphemus holds the plain,
surveying with a sightless eye.
This tower looms into my sleep
and leaves no room for other dreams.

II. The Plain

Once more I walk upon the plain
beneath that solitary gaze,
where ancient twisted vines yet strive
to bear sweet wine for gods long dead.
My shadow far before me falls,
a darkened path I fear to step.

III. Night

Across the plain, now, night approaches,
stars set shining in her hair,
with dark winds sweeping ling'ring light
away to stain the sunset sky.
Work done, she wraps a purple cloak
and, silent, slips through day's back door.

IV. The Watcher

In empty rooms, a watcher waits
before his window, wondering
that he should care who killed the gods
or mourn the passing of the day
once more beyond the plain of dreams,
then turns, as oft he has, away.

V. The Moon

A silent archer of the night,
the moon must loose her silvered shafts.
She wounds me with an easy grace
until my tears wash clean the day
and, emptied then of all but darkness,
arrows pierce this shieldless soul.

VI. Alone

These shapes about me are not real:
I walk with phantoms such as ever
meet one in the mists of dream
and memory long lost to time.
Dawn lies along the world's edge;
the only shadow here is mine.

VII. The Fool

What random throw of dice has brought
the fool upon his thoughtless quest?
With each step taken, each path chosen,
peril lies beneath his feet.
On the horizon, storm clouds gather,
rising dark against the dawn.

VIII. Birds

The plain of dream lies darkened yet,
for dawn has brought a flick'ring play
of lightning 'round that shadowed shaft;
upon the edge of sight, birds circle,
soaring up the staring sky
to seek their sun, since disappeared.

IX. The Stranger

I walk again where grow the vines;
across the plain, a stranger comes.
He will not look at me; we pass,
for each has his own quest to follow,
wandering before the storm,
with eyes fixed on the distant dark.

X. The Gods

Best had the gods not fashioned man,
deserving neither of this life
nor of the death so near he bars
his door against tomorrow's entry.
Did they dream upon a time
and then forget all they conceived?

XI. The Storm

Despair has brought a storm against me,
raised some vast blind demigod
to stretch his hand above the plain.
Alone, the tower stands in light;
within its darkened rooms does he,
that other, wander as do I?

XII. Truth

Again and yet again I walk
this plain, despite the promises
of comfort found in compromise
and in believing ones own lies;
for truth is sorrow and these paths
lead but a little way, then fade.

XIII. The Sun

The sun has opened wide the day
to scatter sharpened shards of light,
these slender dagger blades that cut
from me still more of what I am.
Another layer stripped away;
someday I yet may naked stand.

XIV. Paths

Too long, my paths have led nowhere,
as I have followed others' faiths
or sought to drink deep of the past
among the stones of streams gone dry.
The way may not be seen; I falter,
searching out tomorrow's door.

XV. The Eye

Still, Cyclopean shadow rises,
seeking with its sightless eye
for wanderers who live with faith
in nothing that has gone before.
A greater eye now holds the plain
in ravenous sunset embrace.

XVI. Reflections

Those questions I must fear to speak
lie answered in a dead god's eyes,
arisen from my dull reflection,
fading to oblivion.
Two mirrors face across today,
returning, each, its endless path.

XVII. The Star

A distant tuneless music asks
how I could hope to understand
truths hidden even from the gods,
as one star rises, dancing dim
above that empty endless waste
where dreams lie restless in their graves.

XVIII. The End

In fevered pilgrimage, I've sought
the doors long shut in dream, yet find
each opens only to this plain.
Eyes raised, once more, behold a tower,
ever there on my horizon,
for I dream and dream again.

At Dawn

The sun does not creep this morning,
but grips the sky, all at once,
in pulses of orange and gold and gray.

The storm is minutes away, revealed
along a doubtful horizon glow,
an intimation of dawn postponed.

Thunder heralds a darkness, wind-hollowed,
to fill with rain and remembrance.
I make coffee and wait.

Chips

I knock these little pieces
from the infinite
and try to assemble them
into something that

might make sense,
should make sense.

Spread them on the table,
take another look—
too much is missing, still.
I shall chip anew

at eternity
tomorrow.

A Journey

The Fool, in quest, must journey perilous, far lands,
Ere he return to hold *The World* in his hands.

Illusion masks the world *The Magician* seeks,
But on the day of *Judgment*, truth then clearly speaks.

Though as a virgin veiled, *The Priestess* must be won,
When given freely, is clothed solely in *The Sun*.

The Empress, all the fruitful day, plays mother's role;
The Moon remains the mirror of her untamed soul.

The Emperor may rule the world in his might;
The Star will ever hold sway in the skies of night.

In seeking God, *The Hierophant* builds high his walls,
To be enlightened only when *The Tower* falls.

In Eden, might The *Lovers* have been without sin;
The fruit of knowledge woke *The Devil* that's within.

All in its path must fall before *The Chariot*,
Till *Temperance* can balance fierce desire with thought.

Mature in wisdom and in *Strength*, man at his peak,
Knows *Death* and change must come to strong as to the weak.

On solitary crags, *The Hermit* guards his light,
For soon *The Hanged Man* must face an eternal night.

Upon *The Wheel of Fortune*, riches may be won;
Yet when it turns no longer, *Justice* must be done.

Oracle

What oracle have I become,
searching my own words for meaning?
Ever closer to speaking truth,
ever more ready to misinterpret.

Apollo has sent me no serpents
to whisper smoke-dreams in my ear
nor has Satan shaken down
the sweet fruits of forbidden knowledge.

These words I pick up are the bricks
to fashion temples of poetry
or to throw through their stained-glass windows.
Don't stand in the way, whichever

I choose; you might catch one but not
my whole building when it tumbles
down. The patterns they leave will
be read by priests so all might be

explained. It is the way
of oracles and poets.

The Garden

We were thrown
from one paradise
to find another
in each other,
in the knowledge
of good and evil,
of life and death.

Lend me your innocence.
I'll plant a crop
in that garden,
to ripen under
an angel's watch.
Will you bring
in my harvest?

A Stillness of the Wind

Comes a stillness of the wind.
Down rain-shiny streets it comes,
as each light breathes out a name.
Must the traffic whisper so
of the dawn? These pavements yet
need washed clean of yesterday.

Once, you would translate the night
for me, read the moon and stars
like the word of God, epistles
to the heart. I could believe
then. I was a wandering tribe,
seeking prophecy and rain.

Morning's distant murmur hangs
on this stillness of the wind;
I have driven far and would
close my eyes. Might not I find
hours more of night along
streets that sing rain's lullaby?

CROSSING

From the high passes, I spied
your wealth, coveted
all the golden riches
of tower-crowned cities,
dozing through the days.
The sun had sung you to sleep.

I have crossed the mountains.
What legions can you marshal
against my hunger? What
captain knows the truths
a sword writes on the heart?
The conqueror weighs his costs

like fruit in the market, buying
the ripeness of each promise.
There is no cheating such scales
when I name my ransom.
I have crossed the mountains;
I am in your fields.

Soldier of Fortune

I.

I'll craft you a war of carnelian
and spilt promise,
strung upon the golden
hair of children.

Wear it when the wind
has carried my name
away, carried it from even
the ear of God.

II.

The towered clouds once bowed
to you and me;
we were a king and a queen
upon love's throne.

And there was rain that night
and the truth
of summer's heat was told
by distant lightning.

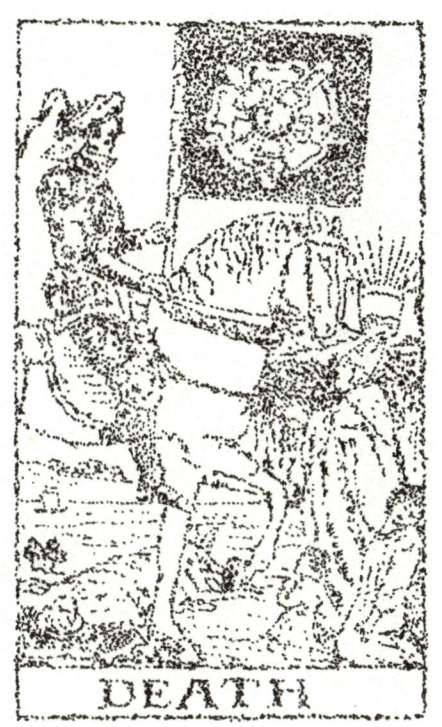

III.

In the bazaar, priests bargain
for misplaced souls,
the cut-rate remainders
no one will read.

Bid me up a little,
won't you? The stacks
of heaven and hell are full
of such already.

IV.

The trees were thick with stars
and tomorrow
when the breeze filled night
with your song.

My heart's become no more
than shadow against
the sky; an urgent wind
has scattered me.

V.

The ink of regret is dark
as the new wine;
drink deeply its promises,
the taste of someday.

I'll craft you a book of moonstone
and desert wind
that only your sleeping eyes
shall ever read.

Horses

I have harnessed up
these dreams of mine.

Here, take the reins,
ride them until they fail.

I will bring to you
fresh horses, tomorrow.

Coinage

I stamped your image
on coins of base metal,
hoping to buy love
from the blind woman.

Whose picture is that?

No one. No one at all.
I only dreamed you,
some lonely night,
a summer night
of the soft moon.

Dreams buy nothing here.

Dream is my currency,
the bright and worthless
coinage of my life.
The sightless
turn them in their hands.

Whose picture is that?

Hers. Always hers.

Dreams buy nothing here.

I know that.

Man of War

Man of war, sleep well to night,
find peace where you lay your head;
the legs of dream may carry you
to dances with the dead.

I'm not the one to judge you, brother,
I'm not the one to ask;
the place to search is your own soul,
Man's solitary task.

You need answer to yourself
only, and your god,
if there are sins to be forgiven,
regrets for paths once trod.

I can not lead you home to rest,
your heart's where that land lies;
man of war, find sleep tonight
and peace when you close your eyes.

Glimpses

Reality and illusion
are the same scene

glimpsed from different
vantage points.

Stand here next to me
and see what I see.

Marches

I have walked the empty marches,
fading light on one horizon
blessed darkness at the other,
welcoming the wanderer.

Crossed again these misted borders,
where desire sings to dream
of my each forgotten hunger;
left the burning lands of life,

gazed upon an endless sea,
vast and black, devoid of promise
save that of eternal peace.
Ah, to sleep in those cold waves,

lulled by wordless, timeless song,
never waking, never waking.
Others drop their burdens here,
ever lost on this lost shore,

slip into oblivion.
No, not yet. I'll walk my dark
only to find light once more;
I can not deny the sun.

It will rise to find me traveling
on the marches of the day.

Listening

I'd fall asleep, listening to her heart
    play my rhythmic lullaby
and measure every breath against my own—
    three for her, two for me.

So sound, so effortless, her slumber seemed
    as I lay listening at her side,
listening to the time flow soft away—
    wishing night could be forever.

Different Stars

We were too crotchety old captains—
wrong, I guess, from the beginning,
each too independent.

Each course set to different stars—
I could have steered my life by yours
had you let me try.

Had you not been so impatient—
you made your turn, corrected course,
leaving me behind.

Leaving me to sail alone—
but I no longer find the stars
above my empty sea.

Answers

I sometimes question all the answers
That I have given to myself,
But can't quite get them sorted out
And put away, each on its shelf.

They disagree with one another,
They squabble over proper place,
And one I think is firmly fixed
Begins to wobble on its base.

For life delights in setting riddles
That trip me up, along my way;
They baffle and distract me so
I'm unsure if it's night or day.

The only thing I know for certain
Is that I'll never truly know
The answers, for they're ever changing:
I must make them up as I go.

Campfire

The stars were the lights
of a Las Vegas casino,
filling the desert night
with promise.

I should have thrown
my last silver dollar down,
anted once again,
even knowing I'd lost.

Faceless dancers faded
to the song of our fire

and each star had
a shining name,
too far away
for us to read.

The world sagged
like a toasted marshmallow;
I had no chocolate
for s'mores.

Look, there are angels—
angels with fiery wings.

Venusburg

Tannhauser, baby—
that's who I feel like lately,
choosing between the sacred
and the profane.
A music seduces, fills
this darkness, this cave,

but even eternal Venus
can't fill a mortal lifetime.
I'm empty. I need more;
more than what we are,
more than being
your sometime lover,

your go-to guy,
the friend-with-benefits.
Sometimes, yeah, sometimes,
baby, I think I'd be
better off alone
than stuck here, halfway

between heaven and hell
and not knowing which
I find in you.

Janitor

a sequence in tanka form

I vacuum this hall
in long swaths, not back and forth
as in the small rooms.
Burnt tuna smell fills the air;
I've sucked up another roach.

Dusting high and low,
my mind wanders here and there,
dreaming many dreams.
I may think I've missed something
but go back to find it done.

I find disorder
or papers in neat stacks by
pictures of children.
I never see these people
but know each one by his desk.

It's a moment's work
to clean dirty coffee cups,
left out once again.
But if I do it this time,
they will always forget them.

Each basket's emptied
into my can and replaced
to hold tomorrow.
Sometimes, an open drink spills;
then I have to rinse it out.

Take care not to bang
into furniture with mop
or vacuum cleaner.
I already get the blame
for enough things around here.

A note will be left
on this desk or that, asking
please do or please don't.
I try to remember who
wants what but usually can't.

Late at night, no one
hears me if I sing at work
or talk to myself.
My voice is good company
in the hours after midnight.

All the doors are locked
when I arrive; I keep them
locked until I finish.
I make my round carefully,
locking myself out again.

Summer's Jewels

The drowsy day is framed by sunlight,
as crisp mid-morning shadows have
become a velvet, cool and blue,
that lines the season's jewel case.

My work, I think, will wait a while;
perhaps tomorrow it may seem
more pressing. But, today, I find
I've wealth enough in Summer's jewels.

The Chance

The lover who is most intriguing
May also prove the most fatiguing;
I need to find a boring someone,
To settle down and soon become one

Myself. Such an unlikely notion!
I love too well all the emotion
Of love and being truly in it;
I'd take the chance this very minute

On living happily ever after
Or finding a few days of laughter
With days of pain, no doubt, to follow—
That same old bitter pill we swallow.

Call me a fool to keep on trying:
To love's to live—I am not dying.

Sophistries

Make sure your bearings in what lands you roam:
The wisest man is he who travels far,
Yet keeps his eye upon a guiding star
That someday serves to show him his way home.

Your hidden secrets, guard and let them sleep:
If honesty's rewards may seem few when
One airs his faults for all to see, know men
Respect those most who their own counsel keep.

Though on uneven ground, tripped by the rules,
We stumble now and then, we need not fall;
For it's a little sin, if sin at all,
And such terrain's the fashioning of fools.

Seek ever for the balance in all things:
Have skepticism without cynicism,
And independence without nihilism;
The freest men are neither slaves nor kings.

Man ever to the future turns his eye,
And must look, wondering, into the distance;
He cannot be content with his existence,
For man's the beast who knows that he must die.

Bankruptcy

How much will you give me for what's left
of tomorrow? It already carries
mortgages I'd never hope to pay.

My heart declared its bankruptcy; my soul
goes homeless on the streets of someone else's
heaven, begging, *Give me a piece of gum*

to stick myself together; I'm crumbling today,
leaving a trail of me wherever I go.

Sink

There are no tides upon the sea of time,
where swimmers stroke the blind still water, dark
caresses carry them yet on in stark
insistent acts of purposed pantomime.
Who spoke to us this languid liquid rhyme
of life that takes some drunken diver's arc
into the deep and leads each to embark,
to journey onward, seeking the sublime?

There rise no tides upon the silent sea;
no subtle currents seek to sway the course
we choose, as destiny is proved to be
only the shadowed mirror to our force.
See how the moon is drowning! Are you free,
oh swimmer? Sink; sink slowly to your source.

Wave Song

Down liquid, lucent halls of flight,
Through splashing, crashing walls of light,
My passions guide me, raise me up
And deep into the crystal cup.

The cool transparent veils I part
To seek her steaming hollow heart,
For oceans can not slake my thirst
Until these deepest wells are burst.

A wizard in his secret cave,
A mystic in his sacred nave,
I enter there to learn my worth,
To die within and find rebirth.

This fragile instant I embrace
Eternal woman's sea-green grace;
The hurled spear I stand astride,
Then laugh as she throws me aside.

If Art Were a Woman

If art were a woman, she'd leave me;
'Wife beater,' she'd tearfully claim.
'He's thrown me about in his anger,
Attacked me with sharp palette knives.
Oh, how my poor canvas has shredded!
And I only sought to give love.'
Yet ever she has returned to me,
Poor, battered muse, luggage in hand,

To tell me that I can do better,
Be my inspiration and nag.
We will fight again and again,
Then make up with passion and paint,
My brush bringing color to canvas—
The studio's filled with our children.

Clytemnestra

When, these long years ago, her husband left,
she grieved; she grieves again at his return
for what must be. A poor return indeed
for Agamemnon and a poor return
for her deed, yet much better than were she
to give him welcome with unloving arms.
These squandered years passed loveless, husbandless,
her thoughts turned to dark vengeance for his sin,
his bloody sacrifice: their daughter dead
and by the very hand of he who once
had cradled her when she, a babe, would cry.

Amytis

Here, there are no mountains,
no tall-treed valleys of shade
and rest. No streams run laughing
beside us, laughing at us

and our love-making. Once,
we knew such laughter, mingling
with our own voices' song,
tumbling away. Such youthful,

boisterous rivers are lost
to hearts that fade, fade as
the flowers we left in
the mountains of the Medes.

We are naked, here.
There is no hiding from
the sun, no secrets kept
from night's knowing stars.

Our faces have become
those of the gods who guard
the city gates, the painted
masonry, weary

of their pretense of power,
of vigilance, of life.
Your kingdom squats upon
these plains, bounded in.

Bounded by great rivers
and by great peaks beyond,
Babylon, the mighty,
is my prison. I long,

O, King and Husband, I long.
For the mountains, I long,
for Media, my home.
Here, there are no mountains.

The Grail

I have styled myself a king,
yet I am but knight-errant,
seeking for my holy grail,
my Queen of Cups. She waits
beneath the rainbows of forever.

All foes vanquished, I stand ready;
though my sun set east
today, I have not lost my bearings,
I shall not lose my way—
leagues I've wandered as a fool.

Beneath the rainbows of forever,
she waits with ten cool draughts
for me, for her thirsting knight.
My Queen of Cups, she waits;
she holds the keys to a great kingdom.

Whispers

God speaks to each of us;
alas, that old devil
is right there whispering
in our other ear.

Who is wise enough
to always know which is which?
Who can say: *God told me this*
or *God said to do that?*

You can ask the priest
and he'll have his answers.
You might ask your mother;
she'll have hers as well.

You-know-who whispers
in their ears too. Even Mom's.
Ask your heart; if it
is good, it will know.

It will know the truth,
no matter how many the lies
come whispering to our ear.
It knows the voice of God.

Alignments

Some say we should sleep
North and South;
forces flowing
freely through us,
our internal magnets
lined up with Earth's poles.

Some say we should sleep
East to West;
streamlined bodies
traveling headlong
as the world rotates
at fantastic speed.

Most of us, I think,
do not care;
some how, we stay
put all night,
never letting nature
nudge us from our beds.

Exile

Each night, lest memory fade,
I whisper your name three times:
my empty incantation,
long since grown meaningless.

This, the land of exile,
allows us no regret;
we have burnt our ships
in fear of the dark.

We are the fruit that falls
too soon and never ripens,
that holds its hard and lifeless
heart until all decays.

Each night, lest memory fade,
my mother whispers my name.
Does she remember the face
that once wore the word?

The Land of Small Demons

A constant sky holds tomorrow
in place, holds it like a careless
glove, toying with its mate,
only to drop it along the way.

In the land of small demons, the days
are taken by the crimson hills.
Behind the sun, beneath the moon,
jackals dig for the ragged scraps.

A great king crossed here once and claimed
all as his realm. His treasury
could not hold the restless sand
nor the stars of a desert night.

Three jewels sing in tree-top, envy
of the silent stone forest.
The small demons are nimble; they climb
in search of their shining eggs.

A poet wandered over thirsty mountains,
full of songs to an unknown love.
Far away, where the day
meets the sky, does she still wait?

Gasping across the dust, mermaids
flop toward their land-locked pools.
Alas, the demons drank them all
and pissed them into the fiery sea.

This treasured pain I wrapped in shadow,
narrow behind me. The little demons
grasp for it; they have taken
my eyes as tokens for their games.

I hear them gambling, casting lots
over empty egg-shells. Discarded
as useless, come dawn, how shall
I find them in the endless sands?

The coupling of gods and men has left
both weary and neither satisfied.
None rest in the land of small demons.
None heed the singing of the jewels.

Look up to the mountains, your distant borders.
Do streams flow there, cool waters of life
and forgiveness? It is not far.
I've heard their song. It is not far.

This Thing

This thing
you want from me—
I used to have it,
would share it
for the asking.

Then I gave it
and it was never returned.
This thing
you want from me—
I don't have it now.

Divides

The rocky divides of God
no longer fence us. We
grew our wings. We saw

that sky is but ocean turned
upside-down and any
deep-blue depth may be sailed.

On what tent-poles have
we hung the mountains, now?
What clouds sing onto

the valleys? We remain
unknown. We whisper across
the heights of each divide.

Wolf

The moon's a mirror; each dog sees
himself as wolf framed in its breadth,
full-waxed into the nameless night.
Which of us might look up and howl

at our own image, true yet distant?
Which of us might believe the day
no longer, trusting only dim
reflections of our soul's desire?

Give me the sun, too bright to look
upon, too much to understand,
a mirror only unto God.
The wolf may sleep in shadowed den,

in dream alone to know the moon
and sing his image from the sky.

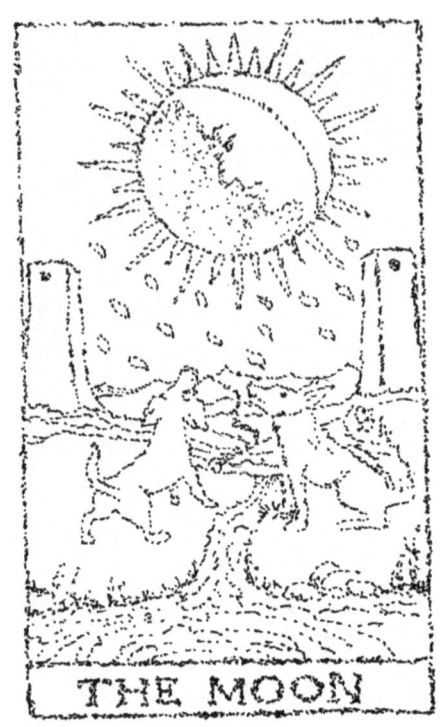

Evening Star

Are you the first star of evening, come
to grant my wish? Unexpected,
you have risen above my horizon;
unlikely, you shine against my night.

Were I a sailor, I would steer
by your bearings. Were I a shepherd
I would imagine angels in attendance
to your light and, following their song,

seek tomorrow's king. But, alas,
I have neither ship nor sheep,
only a great many wishes. I know
you can not grant them, my Evening Star.

I know you shine so I may aspire
to hold the beauty of the night.

The Moon and the Stars

The moon and seven stars
crowd the frame of night.
They knock at the glass,
calling, *come play.*
No, little stars,

I do not fly anymore.
No, Miss Moon, I have grown
tired. My fingers are clumsy;
my voice no longer climbs
the high, thin clouds.

Once, I sang duets
with the summer sky.
Once, she dreamed in my arms
to that music, intoxicated
by the wind's dark wine,

and we danced but never
filled the pauses
in each other's song.
I could only give her
the moon and the stars.

Morning Star

Lonesome is the Morning Star,
last to fade, alone at dawn
but knowing a faint taste of day,
the first bird song, the little lights

that come to life in darkened houses.
So like the stars of night, they are,
her many sisters shining high.
She goes to join them now, farewell,

little lights, little stars
that shine below. Farewell, she fades.

Orphan

Was it you who left
tomorrow at my door,
then ran away?
She lay crying in a shabby basket
and though it broke my heart,
I sent her off to the orphanage
to live with yesterday.

Emptiness

The great emptiness
visited me, whispering
wordless taunts.

Before shone the first
stars, the gods decided
you and I

would come and go,
live and die, be
and be not.

Their laughter is but
an echo, a shadow of
the big bang,

as they, too, have gone
into the empty dark
that lies between us.

My Companion

Every day since—
since I can't remember.
I was nine? Eight?
Maybe younger.
It has been my companion;
every day I have thought of it.

The ending.
The ending of life,
the ending of all,
that dark hole in which
I could hide forever.

It has whispered to me:
Come. Come.
Embrace sweet suicide
and have done with it.

I've never trusted this companion
though we have traveled together
down all my roads,

and sometimes I have listened
all too eagerly.

All too eagerly.

Stairs

Alone is hating the world and yourself,
forgetting that life once seemed to have meaning.

Alone is being far from all you ever
cared for, a gun held trembling to your head.

I think I have a pretty good idea
what hell is like; I walked through there to find

the stairs that led up, up again to the light.

My Companion II

So, you have returned, my old companion.
I thought you long gone. Once you spoke
to me in the sleepless dark, offering rest.

Once I listened; yes, I listened all
too eagerly. I'll walk with you again,
a mile or two; then with polite regret,

turn aside. Your house is not mine
nor can I enter the room you keep ready.

Canyons

The night can be too dark,
the lights far too bright,
to bear either long.

Seek the twilit street;
such dreaming shadows wait
in the heart of the city,

where fitful sleep may sigh
behind the open windows.
Might we find our truth

under some dim street-light,
in the flicker of neon
left burning through the dark?

These ways stand emptied of day,
of all their meaning, canyons
of refuge, of forgetting

when nights may grow too dark
and lights become too bright.

The Court

Four Queens attend me: queens of earth and air,
of fire and water, ladies dark and fair.

Their eyes behold the every turn of fate.
Four youthful Pages at their sides await,

alike unto their mistresses in dress
and face, with wisdom theirs in no way less.

Four Kings most proud and mighty here hold sway,
just rulers yet hard men of war are they.

The elements must serve their each command.
With armored Knights of number same they stand,

their weapons and their tools beside them ever,
to see and know and act, to bind, to sever.

My Court, with staff and sigil, cup and sword,
does guide where I would stray, protect and ward,

advise most wisely when I know but doubt.
Though none might see what destiny deals out,

these images, these lords and ladies play
their game of choice and chance and come what may.

Good Intentions

I know those good intentions
that line your road to hell;
you tarted up your hatred
and sent her out to sell
her body to the lusters
after a virgin whore.
They close their eyes and claim
they've not seen her before.

I know those good intentions,
I know you pray each night
and give thanks to your god
for telling you what's right.
Tomorrow is an apple
that hangs in paradise;
Adam takes a bite
and Abel pays the price.

I know those good intentions—
they line your road to hell.
We've traveled it too often,
we know our way too well
to still mistake the flames
for the rising sun.
Forgive our good intentions,
Lord, when journey's done.

Incognito

God travels in disguise;
we miss Him,
thinking *God's not here,*

God was not there.
But He is.
And He was.

What if God walked
up to you right now
and said, *Howdy?*

I've had My eye on you, He'd say,
but you never noticed Me.
Would you buy His pickup line?

Would you know Him then?

Fool

I fight for faith, I fight and fail,
and still I fight again each day;
a fool, perhaps, a fool who will
neither believe nor disbelieve.

Between faith and despair I hang,
unable to choose hell nor heaven;
a fool, no doubt, to doubt my worth,
my life. Ah, would I were God's fool.

Let Them Go

The night swallowed stars
like sugar in strong coffee
until the skies swam
in storm, and darkness

conversed with the wind.
Could you make out the words?
Did our names become
leaves upon the gale?

Let them go.

How long could we believe
the hidden stars yet shone?
How long could we offer
our hearts to the sightless sky?

The night swallowed the scraps
of yesterday, each spent,
hoarded passion loosed
from a wearied grasp.

Let them go.

I summoned all my dreams
for you, became your hero.
I bore the very lightning
of my soul to you,

brought down my guarded towers.
I am spent; I have
thrown myself away.
The night has swallowed me.

Let me go.

An Old Thing

New for the sake of new
is worth less, even,
than old for the sake of old.

Old, at least, has endured;
that must have value.
Someone, sometime, said

This is good; let's keep it,
and put it away,
saved for our rainy days.

Days when new won't do:
they always come.
Then we search our dressers,

our shelves, our memories,
and there it is,
tucked safely in a drawer,

an old thing that belonged
to Aristotle
or Aunt Dotty, once.

Hill-Farm Sketches

1. July

July was heat and thunder
with an ice-cold creek
flowing through the middle.

2. Hills

Each pine on sandstone hills
knew the soft caress
of a summer moon.

3. Hollows

The oft repeated name
of the whip-poor-will
filled the shadowed hollows.

4. Full

The dogs ate boiled potatoes
when our pockets were empty
but the garden was full.

5. Climb

I could never climb
high enough in the maple
to see all I desired.

6. Voice

The voice of the night
still whispers among the hills
but I can not hear the words.

Forest Lake: Sunset

When golden haze
hangs upon
a hidden horizon,
I linger by the lake.

The forest, dressed
in fiery finery,
looks into its
liquid mirror.

The scarlet maples
in glimmering water reflected,
the setting sun's
red repeated.

There, a leaf falls:
golden ripple,
spreading rings,
flicker and are gone.

The drone of insects,
the splash of feeding fish,
fades with dusk
as all grows calm.

Somewhere, I hear
wings in the dark,
the call of the whip-poor-will
deep in the forest.

The Passing of Time

When I was younger, I was the better man:
What I would, I did; I no longer can.
Age brings reflection and caution is the rule;
Am I now wiser or am I a fool?

When I was younger, sure of my decisions,
I loved without doubts, I trusted my visions.
I see them less clearly the higher I climb,
For vision grows faint with the passing of time.

When I was younger, the roads all ran true;
The passing of time shows how little I knew.
My roads all led nowhere, my truths became lies;
My world is fading before open eyes.

When I was younger, the meanings were clear;
I faced the future with nothing to fear.
Somewhere my life lost all reason or rhyme,
When vision grew faint with the passing of time.

Run

Howl with me tonight, before the moon
wanes again to nothing. Howl into
the heavens so God remembers why he made us,
so we remember why he made us. I'll run

as far as tomorrow with you. Let the next day
find itself, even as the moon diminishes
into a hole among those stars that man,
in all his hubris, once chose to name.

Come and Go

I have learned not to miss you, lately.
Each day, each hour, I fill
my life with little things.
There is the garden. One might

lose himself there, among the rows,
tending to ones mindless chores
beneath the slow clockwork of the heavens.
Never mind that you loved the flowers

and the sunlit days we shared.
Such will come and go, come and go
as you did, and who might stop them?
There is rain tonight. It also

comes and goes, and that is expected.
Tomorrow, I know I shall still yearn
but not so much. I have learned
not to, lately; learned not to miss you.

Hunters' Moon

Dark pines rise into the night,
edged with silver air
and winter's promise, crisp and keen
and chilling, as I fare

into this land where mountains grow
beneath the Hunters' Moon.
The thin clouds race across the sky;
the wind's a mournful tune.

Higher up, there lies a valley,
hollow as my heart,
hungry as the mouths of lovers
knowing they must part.

Forest stands as walls around
these paths, the moonlit rime
glistening like Heaven's stars,
all come to light my climb.

Does a lonesome lake still hold
its mirror to the sky
amid the tall viridian pines
that know the wind and sigh

to feel its careless, cold caress?
Would I hear the call
of the Great Horned Owl that hunts
and haunts across night's fall?

I knew a cabin, once, now dark
and empty as my soul,
when love and Summer was our world,
when my heart was whole,

and all I am and was still waits
there in reflections deep.
Now, the frost lies on this land;
my way grows ever steep.

To look into those depths again
and deeper yet, I seek,
and rest where I once knew myself,
where only life would speak.

Dark pines stand in silhouette
against ascendant light;
beneath the Hunters' Moon I find
remembered trails of night.

Fogs

When we wake from our dream
shall we curse the dawn?

The sun has not seen the things
of the night. Forgive him

when he sweeps away the fogs
that would cling to day.

Pebbles

I have no words beyond these hollow prayers,
these markers in my book of life-goes-on.
Take them, anyway; none better come.
These are the words I have. All else is gone.

Each familiar platitude is worn
like pebbles in a stream. The water flows
onward, downward, to the distant sea,
but writes upon the stone all that it knows.

I should have more words. They too have run
off to the ocean, hidden there among
drowned cities built of alabaster poems
when language was still new upon man's tongue.

Let them go. They left me as I slowed,
forgot the names I gave them in my youth.
What remains will do, must do; they are
my polished pebbles tumbling toward the truth.

The High Places

I shall climb your mountains,
stand upon the high
holy places. Will you
see me then? Will you
hear my voice ascend
the crystal stairs of heaven?

Stars and planets write
prophetic runes above:
Let me know the paths
beyond their constant paths,
learn your silent ways
through the beautiful void,

an empty universe.
Ah, this dark energy
carries every prayer
away; random angels
sleep behind my sky.
Is this enlightenment?

Are these my excuses,
my reasons to exist?
Time has no song but this,
sung on the high places.
I have learned and lost it
too many times already.

STONE

Unlike Sisyphus,
I, someday, shall sleep
in the shadow of my hill.

Let this stone then stand,
speechless sentinel,
at my head, companion still,

marker of the grave
where I, weary grown,
lie forgetting want or will.

WALLS

These walls between life and death
grow thin. Some nights, the muffled noise
of eternity wakens her,
whispers from another room.

Most of yesterday is lost
in that murmured cacophony,
her husband's voice, the names of the dead.
Where has her husband gone? He slept

at her side a moment ago.
Each memory's become a sheet
of paper, torn and reassembled,
pasted into random collage.

Again, she listens, puts her ear
to these walls. Ah, those voices:
she should know them, but why has someone
replaced the photos that once hung there?

Replaced them all with strangers and echoes
of old songs. Who will dance now?
Who will hold her when the walls
between life and death grow thin?

Deconstructed Piano

The deconstructed piano plays every song
written. Its strings have been removed.
They coil in their boxes, waiting to strike.

I can sit and count the blacks and the whites
and know they are not enough. Sometimes
and some things will always come.

Or else they were always here. What melody
might I concoct if I knew the reason
a piano is? Would you listen?

Cherry wood leans against the wall, waiting
for itself. It knew every song written,
once. It will sing them to the fire.

No Wine Before Its Time

Love and wine—
as they mature,
the flavor must change,
their taste become
that of vinegar
or of heaven.

Would you drink
only of the new
for fear of those
sour remnants?
The finest vintage
needs its time.

Syrah

There is a bottle of Syrah,
breathing out its deep-red dreams
in the dark of the spare bedroom.
We should use it or it will spoil;

the wine, that is, though you are welcome
to the room as well. You know
that, right? Just chase the cats off the bed.
It would be good to have you here

a while, to share the evening, the wine.
I've never asked for more than this;
I have not sought you as a lover
nor seen you as a lover. Oh, maybe

in my own secret deep-red dreams
I have breathed you out, allowing
the bouquet to linger, fragile
as tomorrow morning's goodbyes.

The Climb

The mountain was a morning's climb,
now I stand at the peak;
my way winds down from here into
the valley each must seek

for rest when our ascent is done
and weary, we return
to lay our head, to close our eyes,
to no longer yearn.

I might touch the stars from here,
before I must descend,
but I know they will stand their guard
as I sleep and mend.

A mountain is a morning's climb,
then comes long afternoon
and dreams before a warming hearth
and life's fading tune.

Women and Birds

Dawn sang to me in the voices
of women and birds.

The robins will all fly south
to return some spring morn.

Does love ever again seek
the nest it once knew?

River

This river marks my border;
its voice is umber depth
and whispers. Go no further,
it tells me. Here you end.

My lands encompass leagues
of day—a pilgrim's realm,
a kingdom of the sun.
I covet those that lie

beyond the flood. I seek
those countries of the moon,
the silvered, silent stars,
the sea at river's end.

This river marks my border;
no, I shall not cross over
today. I have my realm,
my kingdom of the sun.

Coin-Toss

Everyone deserves
a second chance but I
have never asked for one,
never would ask for one.

Come. Let us tell
the full moon of our regrets;
let us sing until
morning learns the tune.

Then, what is, will be;
each decision sleeps
off its drunken coin-toss
and wakes with no regrets.

Innocent

A naked innocent, playing
in the garden—so I was,
so I was, until you whispered
of a gate. I know now

what lay beyond. Let me once more
sleep with Paradise's peaceful
beasts, each as I named it, and forget.
Within me grows a forest; the seeds

I carried forth rooted themselves
and everywhere the fruit of knowledge
rots upon the branches. Who
can hope to pick them all? I have

eaten and spat out the taste
of memory. How else can
I live here? How else can
I die a naked innocent?

Babel

I have built, stone by stone,
word by rough-hewn word, my tower
to reach God. He hides behind
the sun. He writes upon the clouds

in runes a thousand tongues have
murmured without understanding.
Another inch, another word—
I seek him in this labor yet.

Come dwell a while in Babel; dwell
with me and we shall name the streets
anew each day. See them, laid
in line and page below us, confusion

singing among the empty houses.
Everyone has come to climb
the stair, look toward whatever heaven
they hope to hide within their hearts.

I extend my hand to him
once more and find myself, as ever,
lacking, my way grown longer but
no closer. Gaze upward, measure again.

My scaffolds must remain about me,
testimony to this toil,
blasphemy and poetry
working ever hand in hand,

until my hand might grasp the sky
and shake tomorrow loose. Give me
only a place to stand, a higher
place, a tower to reach God.

For more from Stephen Brooke – poetry, novels, children's books
– please visit the Arachis Press
http://arachispress.com

www.ingramcontent.com/pod-product-compliance
Lightning Source LLC
Chambersburg PA
CBHW051713040426
42446CB00008B/869